nothing
by Ideas with Ink

A Noveltry
(Novel + Poetry)

101 Panya Publishing
101panya@gmail.com
ISBN 13: 978-1-988880-06-8
ISBN 10: 1-988880-06-8

Dedications:

To nobody:

{To somebody}

<To anybody>

[To everybody]

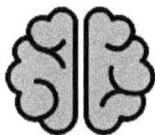

Pre-preface:

War killed peace because peace

tried **to start a war.**

Pre😀 :

My name was murdered. In its

next life, it became my identity.

TABLE OF CONTENTS

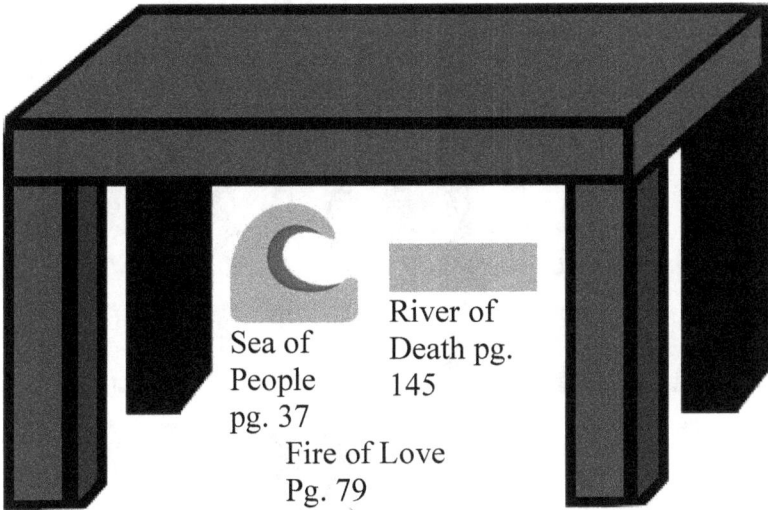

We/are/born/In/a/star.

There are 2 stars that we can see from Earth:

Star-dom and **Star-vation.**

For every person that sees

Star-dom: ,

and many **more** see Star-vation.

A movie studio wanted to make the Movie of Life.

(thanks to a word bank):

the, studio, built, the, universe

There was no color in the universe, so the studio hired Life to paint it. He found all the colors in two places:
His mind and heart.

Life walked to his mind. He entered a black market in a gray area. He bought a blue collar and a green belt. He tried to steal a shrinking violet, but got caught with red hands by Agent Orange. He brown nosed the Agent and threw the violet into the *"white trash". Life walked back to his heart because his yellow belly hurt. There, he discovered a pink slip in a pile of black mail.

*used metaphorically (since life is a metaphor and love is a simile). **No people are trash.**

Then, Life painted the whole
universe (different colors) (including people).

The studio auditioned 12
directors for the Movie of Life.

Director:	Random Fact
L-o-v-e	o:-)(a-n-g-e-l)
Hope	+O:-)(pope)
Time	-=#:-) (wizard)
Destiny	Q:-)(college grad)
Lust	:|] (robot)
Fear	:0) (clown)
Power	(:| (egghead)
Fame	:^)(liar)
Hunger	:() (loudmouth)
Thirst	%*} (drunkard)
Greed	$-) (gold-digger)
Hate	>:) *(devil)*

The movie studio created 7 planets and hired 7 directors for the Movie of Life.

On the Grey planet:
The studio hired Time.
Chess pieces = inhabitants
Year 1: The **white pieces** and the **black pieces** had grey kids.
Year 2: Everybody realized they were the same color.
Year 3: They all
                        jumped off the chessboard.
Year 4: The studio fired *Time.*

On the Orange Planet:
The studio hired Lust.
Lego pieces = inhabitants.
Year 1: The Lego pieces built a city segregated by color
Year 2: One day, they hosted the life Olympics…

Results in the life Olympics:

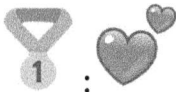

… and when the Lego pieces tried to
lift their dreams   their hearts broke
    (*1 peace became 7.5 billion pieces*)
Year 3: The studio fired **Lust.**

On the Yellow planet:

The studio hired Hope.

Rubber Ducks = inhabitants.

Year 1: The *lame ducks* killed all the ~~ugly ducks.~~

fly.

Year 2: The *lame ducks* died trying to

Year 3: The studio fired Hope .

On the Blue planet:

The studio hired Fear.

Dominoes = inhabitants

Year 1: They made a l-i-n-e to get into the box (that

society built), except the odd ones.

Year 2: The odd ones died from the cold outside the box. The even

ones died from the heat inside the box.

Year 3: The studio fired Fear.

On the Red planet:

The studio hired Love.

Cards = inhabitants.

Year 1: The face cards made a

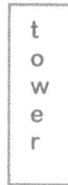

t
o
w
e
r

.

The number cards made a pyramid.

Year 2: The cards became things not people.

Year 3: The studio fired L-o-v-e.

On the Green planet:

The studio hired Greed.
Battleships = inhabitants.

Year 1: The relation-ships enslaved the friend-ships.

Year 2: The relation-ships were eaten by self-fish.

Year 3: The friend-ships were eaten by loan Sharks.
Year 4: The studio fired Greed.

On the Gold planet:

The studio hired Destiny.

Snakes and ladders = inhabitants.

Year 1: Snakes lived with snakes and ladders with ladders.

Year 2: They built a nuclear-family power plant.

Year 3: When a snake fell in love with a ladder the power plant exploded.

Year 4: Family trees of all kinds grew after everybody died.

Year 5: Destiny chopped down the family trees and sold them to make lust fires*.

Year 6: The studio fired **Destiny.**

*straight/non-straight wires can also make lust/love fires.

11

Every planet ended in death, so the studio hired Life. Life got a blue-green planet. And he created Earth.

Is the world

an oyster Or a Venus flytrap?

Then. Then. Then. Then. Then.
Life. Life. Life. Life. Life. Life.
Life. Life. Life. Life. Life. Life.
changes. changes. changes.
changes. changes. changes.
changes. changes. changes.
his. his. his. his. his. his. his. his.
his. his. his. his. his. his. his. his.
his. his. his. his. his. his. his. his.
his. his. his. his. his. his. his. his.
name. name. name. name. name.
name. name. name. name. name.
name. name. name. name. name.
to. to. to. to. to. to. to. to. to. to. to.
to. to. to. to. to. to. to. to. to. to. to.
Death. Death. Death. Death. Death.

Love is red
Hope is yellow
Fear is white
God is brown
Death is black

Love is human
Hope is human
Fear is human
God is human
Death is human

You are everybody in your mind
and anybody in your heart.
You are everybody in your mind,
but is anybody in your heart?

14

Life for minds:

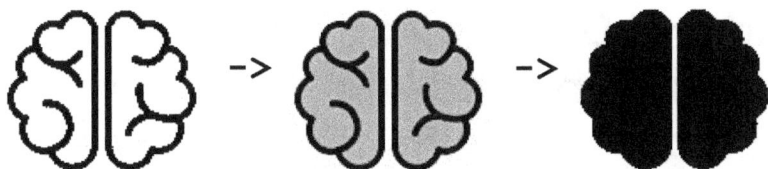

Life for hearts:

Life for souls:

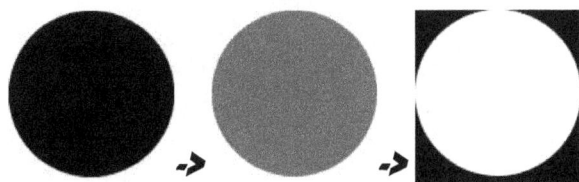

God and Death are drowning in the sea of people. Neither of them can swim, so they are holding to each other.

God and Death climb onto a citizen-ship filled with immigrants, but it crashes with an iceberg of bigots. The ship survives and continues sailing, but the iceberg doesn't and breaks up.

Then, the sea of people begins to dry up:

Workhorses are slaughtered.

"Aliens" are forced to go home.

Plastic people melt.

The images you are trying to view do not represent the true beauty of humans.

Whosever is left in the sea of people splits up by the color of their skin and 5 seas are created: the black sea, the brown sea, the red sea, the white sea, the yellow sea.

God and Death disembark the citizen-ship and walk into a forest made up of family trees and flowers of love.

(Family trees and flowers of love compete for survival.)

L

U   π

🧠   *is the l*   *of a brain-pla*ne 🙂

S   o

T   t

hateisthe 😠

DRIVER OF A

PAIN   TRAIN

              A
          L   T
      E 💚 I
    R 💚💚 on   😍
Start: S

L   H   a

O   I   F

Ve   P   O

IS the CAPTAIN

18

We grow the tree of life.

We cut down the

tree

of

l

i

f e to make the fire of love.

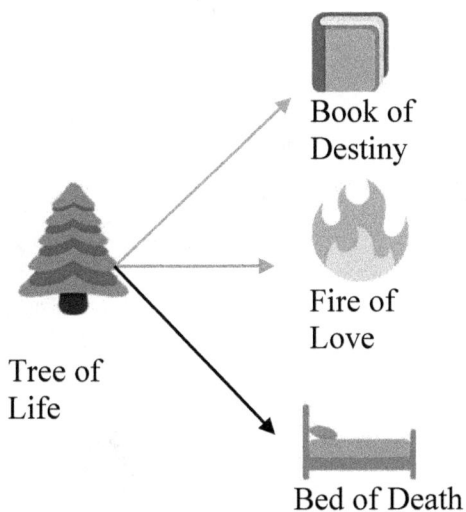

Book of
Destiny

Fire of
Love

Tree of
Life

Bed of Death

Different Tree Species

Poul-tree

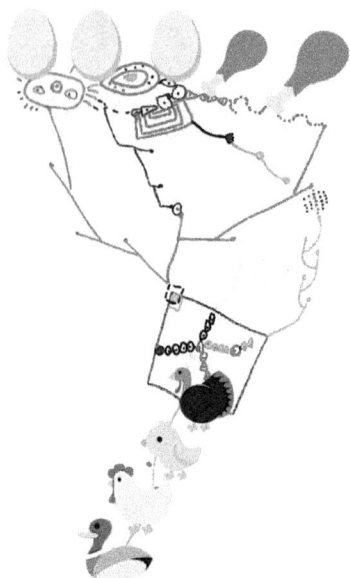

Geome-tree

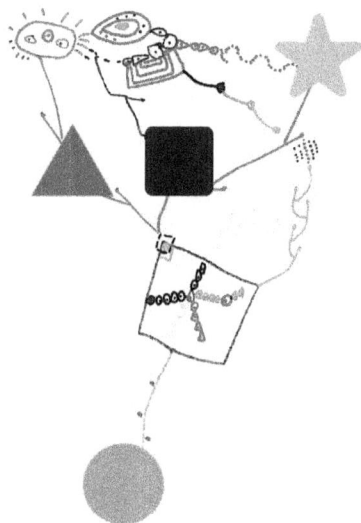

Coun-tree

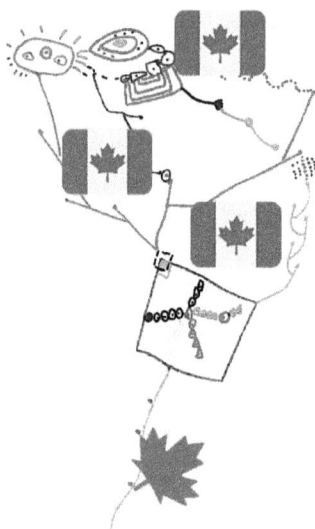

Bigo-tree

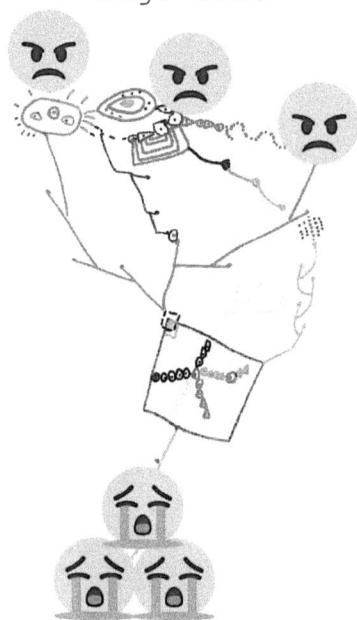

IN THE FOREST, GOD AND DEATH FIND THE TREE OF LIFE. GOD CHOPS IT DOWN AND MAKES A DOOR OF LIFE. DEATH OPENS THE DOOR AND FINDS A CINEMA. THERE, GOD AND DEATH BECOME STUCK IN THE IRON CURTAIN BENEATH THE WINDOW TO THE WORLD. AFTER 1991 MINUTES, THEY MANAGE TO GET OUT. DEATH & GOD WATCH THE MOVIES/ 💔 COMMERCIALS OF THEIR LIVES. DURING BOTH, THEY BOTH FALL ASLEEP.

Every **life** is **a** tragedy, **a** comedy, **a** drama,

a horror,

and **a** romance.

💔

love is a commercial

during the movie of life

If I + I **= window**

And U + U = mirror

Then,

I + U = door

Further along, in the forest, they find the flower **of love.** Death picks the flower and finds a window under it. Death and God go through the window and discover a **SHOE-STORE**.

They are locked in a closet with
two STRAIGHT-FACED MASKS.

Society comes in and gives them a pop quiz:

Quiz: T/F

__1. There is no such thing as a walk-in closet.

__2. There are no monsters in the closet: only people.

(Answers: Both are true).

They both get all the answers right. After **2015 minutes, society lets them out.** God **and** Death try on all 7.5 billion pairs of shoes. **Barefoot, they leave.**

We rent **Ap art me nts** in each other's eyes before

we buy h**oUSe**s in each other's **heartS**.

God moves into an **Ap art me nt** in Death's **eyes**.

There is a leak.

Death buys a h**oUSe** in God's **heart**.

There is no heat.

God and Death drink emotions and eat dreams.

Then, they eat frozen emotions and drink liquefied dreams.

We ARE

dreams **not**

~~dreamers.~~

One day when it rains night-mares: ( ),

Death closes the door [ ] to God's heart

And walks to the sea { } of people.

He becomes a ( ) erman there.

Death sends God this text message:

> I cast my dream-net into the sea of people, but get nothing, except my past self.

God replies:

> Death is dead (to me).

I'm not shallow.
You haven't dug:

deep
enough.

Death floods the **apartment** God lives in. She abandons his **eyes** and finds <u>memory lane</u>.

Dreams are buses (🚌🚌🚌) on <u>memory lane</u>. God walks into the dream-bus station.

In the station, there are:

- a stained-glass ceiling*

  a glass ceiling

- a bamboo ceiling/an adobe ceiling/a mud ceiling/a hide ceiling

- a cotton ceiling [⚧]

- a dyed cotton ceiling [⚧⚧⚧⚧]

*even goddesses have glass ceilings. even people have glass ceilings.

Turn the world upside-down

and you will be   above

the glass ceiling.

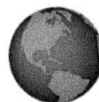

Thor is standing next to God. He is hammered. She steals his hammer and breaks every ceiling.

1920 minutes later (.x3)

Twelve dream-buses go by.

One with people with red hearts who kill dreams.

One with people with green hearts who rape dreams.

One with people with pink hearts who molest dreams.

One with people with purple hearts who beat up dreams.

One with people with orange hearts who burn dreams.

One with people with blue hearts who drown dreams.

One with people with bronze hearts who bury dreams.

One with people with gold hearts who steal dreams.

One with people with silver hearts who rob dreams.

One with people with yellow hearts who imprison dreams.

One with people with white hearts who evict dreams.

One with people with black hearts who exile dreams.

God boards the 13th bus. Justice is the driver.

Those without a heart: Hate, Fear, Power, Greed, Anger etc. sit in the front, and those with two hearts: Optimism, Equality, Love, God, Hope, Peace, Empathy etc. sit in the back.
Fate, Destiny, and Time (all with one heart) are in the middle.

The bus stops at a pharmacy.

The pharmacy's mission statement is:
Let's make people people instead of races, genders, gender identities. claSSes, sexualities, *illnesses*, f✡✝i hs/r☪li🕉i☯ns, disabilities.

At the pharmacy, there are pills with labels and instructions on how and when to use. Every pill tastes the same, but looks different. Every pill is labeled:

By race:

By gender:

etc.

The white straight able-bodied Christian cis rich man pill is a best seller.

Optimism takes off all labels, throws them in the trashcan of the past, swallows all 7.5 billion pills and **overdoses.**

The next day at the pharmacy only one kind of pill is sold:

a human pill.

On the bus, Power moves to a seat in the back.

The bus drives to an ice cream store.

Everybody buys *two* **vanilla** scoops *and* **a** vanilla dipped *cone* or **two** chocolate **scoops** with **chocolate** dipped **cone except:**

1. Hope who buys **two cones:** one chocolate dipped and one **vanilla dipped.**

2. **Fate** who buys **four scoops** of ice cream: two chocolate **and two coffee.**

3. **Love who buys** two scoops **of strawberry ice cream without** a cone.

4. Time who buys **every flavor:** chocolate/coffee/lemon/strawberry/vanilla) and every kind of cone.

5. Peace who buys a vanilla dipped **cone, but** exchanges it for two scoops of vanilla ice cream in a cup.

6. **Greed** who **buys** nothing.

The store run out of ice cream because the gender-blender broke, so the owners: gender and race, married with a kid named sexuality, converted the store to a melting pot restaurant.

Menu at the Melting Pot Restaurant

Dishes: Melting Pot (with a globe)

Ingredients: tears, liquid money, immigr-ants

Price: GDP of the Earth

(for a smaller portion substitute Earth for a country)

The recipe:

immigr-ants

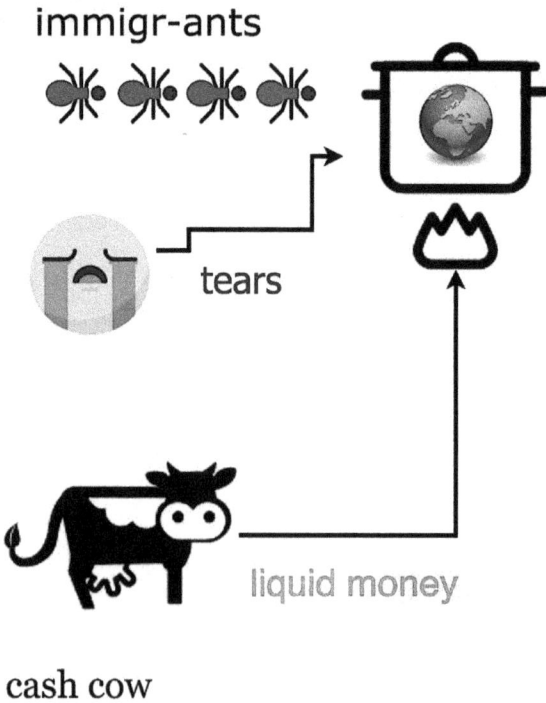

tears

liquid money

cash cow

God orders a MeLting Pot. She sHares it with the other 194 pEople who Are On the bus. They cut up the glObe into unequal pieCes. A few eat with liquid money, some- with both, but most- with tears. They Pay by asking the peoplE who are liVing in their hEarts to donate money. They pay thE bill and they all head back to the bus.

On the highway of life, the dream-bus crashes, because <u>justice is drunk</u> <s>not blind</s>. Everybody waits for the dream-police to investigate, but only

God walks to the garden of Eden.

Random stories about the garden of Eden:

Story 1: Life divided us into:
bananas **apples coconut cacaos** cauliflower,
who were growing on the tree of life until some scientist
named Equality, came and made every human:
a blueberry, since we are all made of water.

Story 100,000,000,000,000:
Society thought we were *fruits*, ~~nuts~~ or <u>vegetables</u>.
But we were sleeping birds, bees and dragons.
When we woke up, we lifted the world, and turned it
upside down.

Tree

don't pick fruits, of <u>nuts</u>,

life vegetables

from the tree of life. THEY DESERVE TO LIVE TOO.
[ALSO, DON'T CALL THEM THAT.]

Today, a friend-ship is Noah's ark.

The predators: 💔 eat 🩶 : the prey.

Today, a relation-ship is La Amistad.

Relationships follow the "love triangle".

Friend-ships are lifeboats on ~~relation-ships.~~

Slave owner: 🧠

Slaves: 🤍🧡🤎🩶🤍🖤🩶🩶🤎

Today, a citizen-ship is the Titanic.

Citizen-ships are made from coun-trees.

1st class: 🩶 2nd class: 🤍 3rd class: 💔

In the sea of people at night only two things light up: love and hope.

Which one you'll see depends on if you're on a

`relation-ship` or a `friend-ship`:

Love

Hope

Friend-ships

are made from

Family trees.

In the garden of Eden,
1. God chops down a family tree

2. And builds a friend-ship

3. With a moral compass.

4. The friend-ship
breaks the ice on the river of death.

5. Crocodile tears eat the friend-ship.

Then:

1. God chops down the tree of life

2. And builds a one-sided relation-ship.

*

3. The   one-sided relation-ship sinks

4. and God escapes on a friend-ship.

Then:

1. God chops down a coun-tree

2. And builds a citizen-ship.

*two faced people have one-sided love.

In the citizen-ship: God sets sails in the 5 seas which are
the black, **white,** red **,** yellow, **&** brown **seas
people created.** God visits all 5, but they are all the same.

Then, people try to be another eye color, so 6 seas form:
hazel purple amber gray blue brown green seas.
God visits all 6, but they are all the same.

Then, in every sea, people begin to cry,
(because they are alone), so 1 sea forms:
the blue sea.

Then, everybody separates by the first letter of their
names. Most letters leave to create the sky, the
mountains, but the H to O names stay behind.
Eventually, people become selfish, so their hearts
become self-fish in the sea. God sails on the citizen-
ship to look for the hearts.

She finds:

1 heart with everything

2 hearts without phone service

3 hearts without internet/phone service

4 hearts without money/internet/phone service

5 hearts without friends/money/internet/phone service

6 hearts without education/friends/money/internet/phone service

7 hearts without family/education/friends/money/internet/phone service

8 hearts without shelter/family/education/friends/money/internet/phone service

9 hearts without food/shelter/family/education/friends/money/internet/phone service

10 hearts without water /food/shelter/family/education/friends/money/internet/phone

You have a job in every heart you visit, since every heart is a society:

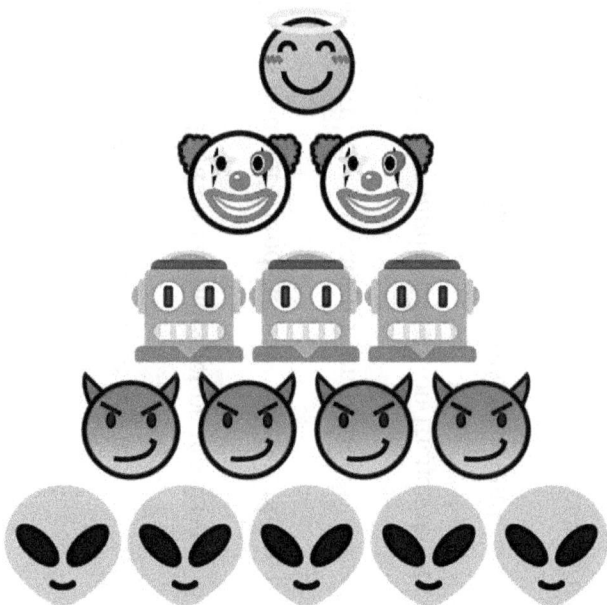

not related to the bottom pyramid

God gives back the hearts, leaves the citizen-
ship and walks up four social ladders.

to upper
to upper middle
to lower middle

to working

From lower

There are four ways to get to Heaven:

1. ramp 2. stairS 3. elevator 4. EScalator

God takes the elevator to Heaven and passes the floors

1. Where people get the weather in their heart.

2. Where people get the size of their heart.

3. Where people get **the material** of their heart.

4. Where people get **the** color of their heart.

5. Where people l-i-n-e up to get the lottery ticket for their next life.

God gets off and waits in that line on the moon.

Everywhere is nowhere but anywhere is somewhere.

nowhere but   nowhere but

anywhere is   anywhere is

somewhere.   somewhere.

To get the winning ticket at the lottery of life, God tries to buy it with Her race card, and then Her w♀man card, but both cards are declined. She uses Her human card

and receives it. and receives it · and receives it. and receives it · and receives it.

You don't need a w♀man/g⚢y/race card to buy a suffer-ring. **You just need a human card.**

God gives the winning ticket to 7.5 billion people, who split it up in 7.5 billion pieces.

None of them can cash their piece in,

because pieces of peace don't equal peace.

God finds a  above Her.

She cuts the silver lining with Her heart & finds a gold heart.

(Gold diggers destroy hearts of gold)

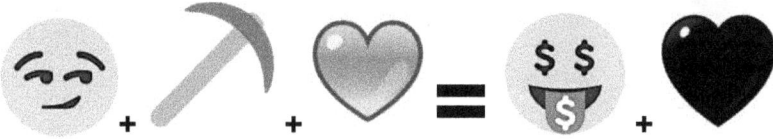

In the heart, God finds a pair of glasses which have no lenses, so God walks to an I-doctor.

Emoji Love story

Eye, sea, yew

Eye, steel, yew

Eye, berry, yew

The I-doctor gives God several colored lenses:

Blue: The world is an aquarium:

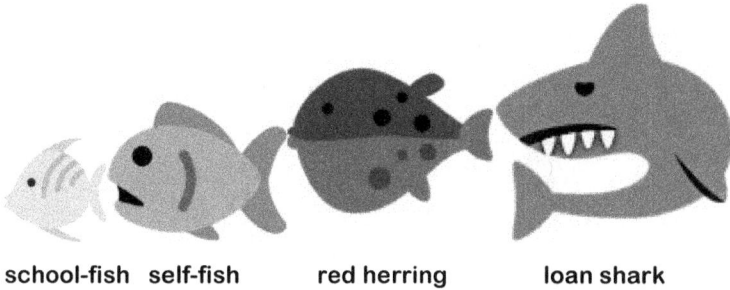

school-fish self-fish   red herring   loan shark

Red: The world is a hospital :

50%:   50%:

Green: The world is a bank

1%:   99%:

She buys the red lenses.

God decides to walk to Her heart.

She stops in Her brain.

On the right side is a dream repair shop.

On the left side is a dream recycling station.

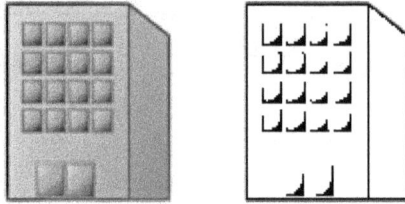

God gives Her dreams to the shop to be repaired.

The shop takes and brainwashes them.

In the dryer, they burn Her dreams.

So, they give God a FREE coat of destiny.

The coat has a hOle in it, and God's life slip

ps away.

Life is a coat: some of us are stuck in the hood.

Life is a coat: some of us are stuck under a blue collar.

Life is a coat: some of us are stuck under a bible belt.

We are nightmares in coats of hope. We are miracles in coats of despair.

The repair shop goes bankrupt because brain-washing doesn't clean a dream, so God walks into the dream recycling station & gives up all Her dreams **to be recycled into thoughts.**

We reduce dreams until we reuse dreams. We reuse dreams *until we recycle dreams.*

Dream recycling:
dreams ->   thoughts ->   nightmares

 ->  ->

God walks on to Her heart following

Her blood stream

She passes by three towns:

1. **Peace, where people consume pieces of pain.**

2. **War, where people eat raw pain.**

3. Indifference, where people snack on the pain of others and call it their own pain.

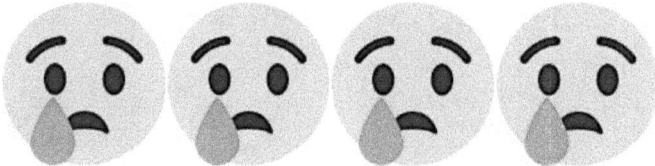

In God's heart, there is a smaller heart.

In **that heart-** a smaller one,
and in **that one-** an even smaller one.
When She reaches the smallest heart, she finds nothing,
except a bunch of stars.

God's heart(s):

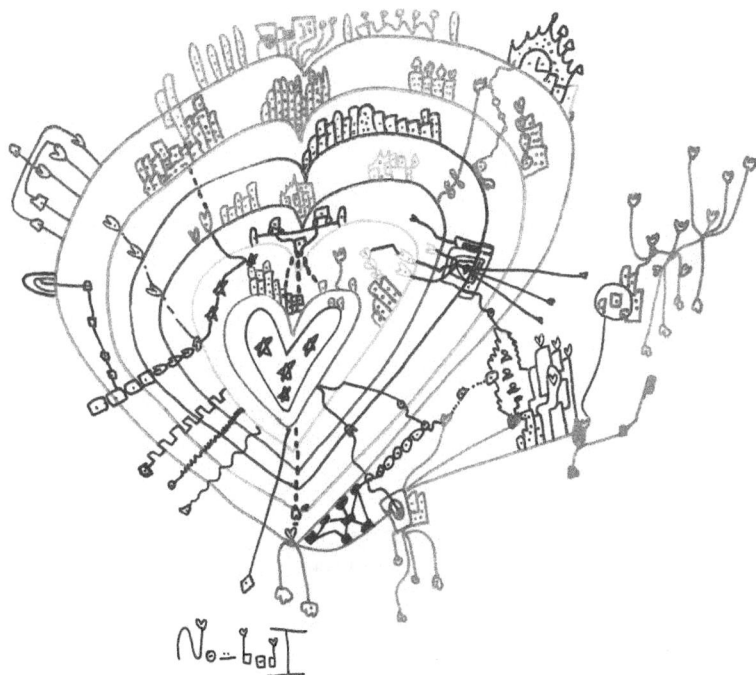

Humans hatch out of stars.

100 people live in 100 stars.

1 guy spends his whole life in a star painting it blue with tears.
99 girls hatch.
86 girls live and die in the
dream/miracle/kiss/smile/heart/**tear** factories.

13 girls, each with a different
colored heart, live and die.
They are the girls with the
white/blue/**green**/pink/purple/
bronze/**silver**/gold/yellow/orange/red/
black/grey hearts.

We use blanket terms when it rains copycats.

We use umbrella terms when it rains underdogs.

99 girls leave the stars in

God's heart and get to the Universe.

99 girls eat clouds with

traffic jam.

(People with their heads in the clouds build castles in the sky.)

86 girls move to factories () on an **ice-cube**. Still hungry, the 13 girls eat the Earth (like an orange removing the peel). They throw the seeds of knowledge into the Universe and which grow into bigo-trees. The orange heart girl hides the peel in her pocket.

You can only lift the

Earth

when you are wearing the

shoes of somebody else.

Earth is bipolar.

vs

God heads back to
the Moon. She takes
out Her heart, places
it on the Moon and
lives in it. In her heart,

God eats
boiled
burned (she burned a bun in the oven.)
frozen
dreams.

The 13 girls walk to an ice-cube. Greed (who is non-binary and uses the pronoun *they*) lives there:

Their heart is a point   ●

They is a line   ──────────

They live*s* in a square house

on an ice-cube.

The girls erase Greed and *their* house.

On every face of the cube there is a
factory, where the 86 girls work in the
dream/miracle/kiss/*smile*/~~heart~~/tear
factories.

On every face of the cube there are
flowers/trees/birds/*butterflies*/~~clouds~~/stars,
where the 86 factory girls live.

The 13 girls put:

thOrNs on

```
      s
 t      a                              a              on
 r  s                              obi    dst
          s                          c      r      s
  w      g
     i   n      on
       ou
  cl  ds.              Moun
```

tains on

```
         bu      tt
              er
         fli     es
```

tree   f 1 o

```
    s                              w
    .                            loc   e
  h   o      on                  ks      r
  S   es                              on      s.
```

The DREAM FACTORY on the ice-cube closes down. Potential, buys it and it becomes **NOTHING** or **everything.**

The TEAR FACTORY
froze/flooded
and becomes a
skating rink/aquarium.

The **KISS FACTORY** becomes a **MISS FACTORY**.

The MIRACLE FACTORY becomes a miracle museum (because miracles go extinct).

The HEART FACTORY begins to make defective hearts (because they are broken).

The SMILE FACTORY starts making FROWNS.

(SMILES are boats for HEARTS.)
(FROWNS are flipped-over SMILES.)

Every human is either

A: a miracle

B: a nightmare

C: a thought

D: a dream

Types of People:

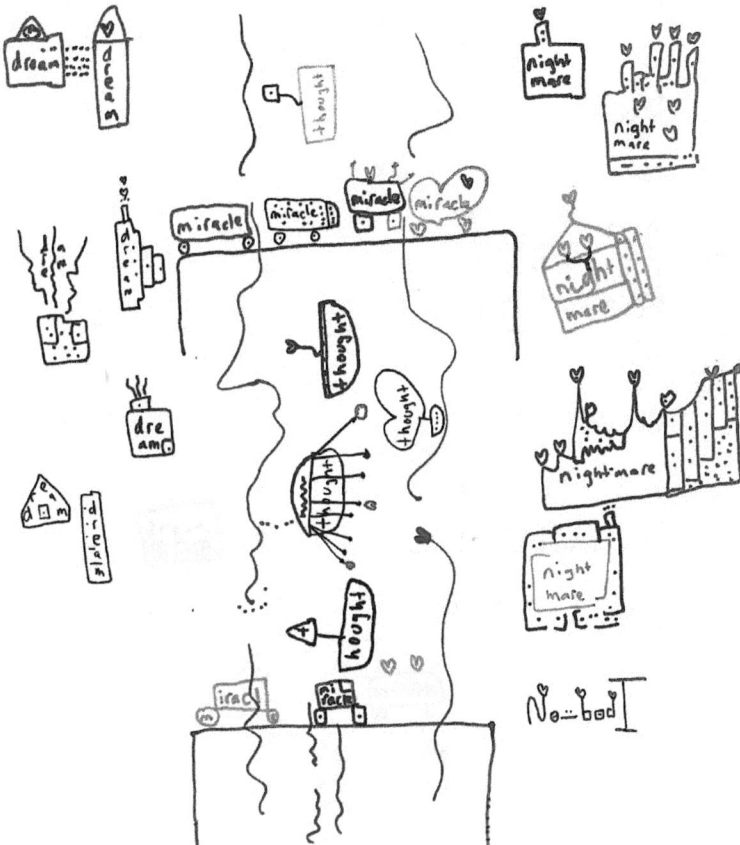

The Diet of Dreams/Miracles/Thoughts/Nightmares:

Dreams:
Food:

Drink:

THOUGHTS:
FOOD:

DRINK:

Nightmares:
Food:

Drink:

MIRACLES:
FOOD:

DRINK:

The factory girls (each with a different color mind) abandon the ice-cube and take the escalator to Heaven. **They use** another escalator, and another one, and another **to get to the top of the** <u>the</u> **Universe which is** <u>the</u> **bottom**/(Hell) of <u>the</u> **next** Universe.

In the new universe's Hell, the 86 girls convert their souls from cars into taxis.

Every soul uses the highway of life. (The soul is a car that runs on dreams).

26 Earth people take a: 8 Earth people take the:

66 Earth people drive a: .

the girl with a Green mind gets a parking ticket which reads:

Color of Soul: Green
Type of Soul: Old
Soul Insurance: Yes

Note the following offences:

1. Using a spot reserved for broken hearts ✓
2. Parking on a prive-ledge
3. Parking in front of a money tree ✓

The girl with the Green Mind drives to the highway of death.

the girl with a Blue Mind gets a parking
ticket which reads:

Color of Soul: Blue
Type of Soul: Stolen
Soul Insurance: no

Note the following offences:

1. Driving a stolen soul
2. Not wearing a bible belt ✓
3. Speeding through life ✓
4. Drinking honest-tea

The girl with the Blue Mind drives on the
Highway of life.

Connect ...

1. 6.   5.   4.

(connect 1-6 and 7-13 separately)

        8.   10.
   7.   9.   11.
  13.

        12.

2.   3.

All the exits on the highway of life:
(Exit # = age)

Note: 1 building represents 1 billion people

Exit 0: city of Life

Exit 2: the child-hood

Exit 16: city of Love

Exit 18: the adult-hood

Exit 25: the parent-hood (not everybody exits)

Exit 30: city of Love (again)

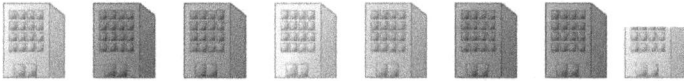

Exit 72: city of Death

Exit 73: Heaven   Hell

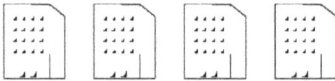 

The girl with the Blue Mind gets off at the exit to Heaven.
The girl with the Blue Mind is suicidal in Heaven.
The girl with the Blue Mind kills herself with a loaded question.

Killing your thoughts
is murder,

but killing your dreams

i

s

u   i

n   c

s   i.

e   d

p

Guilt is a country with many fault-lines.

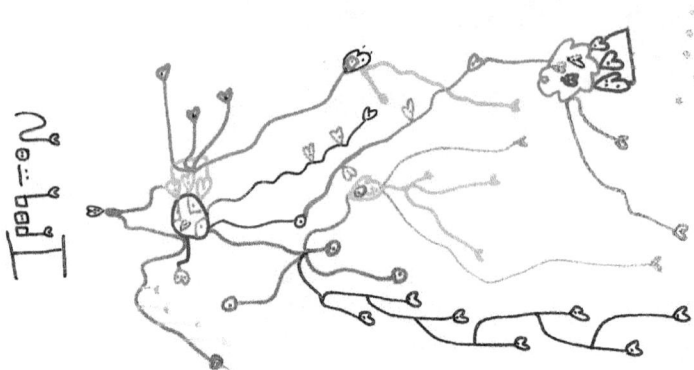

Depression was a country with many valleys

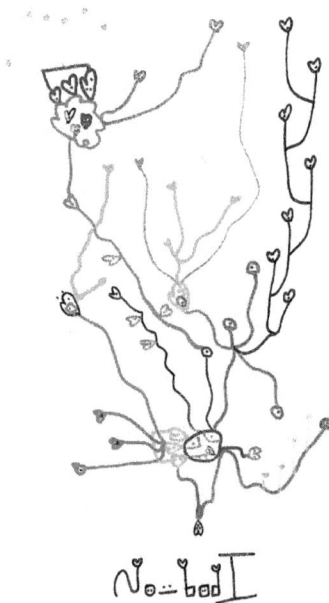

now, Valleys from ~~cuts~~ are now filled with **family** trees

How to create another planet:

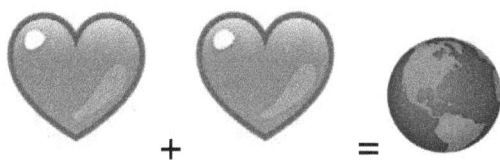

On the ice-cube, the 13 girls create a planet:

They populate their planet in 2 ways:
1. By placing the people and cities from the Earth's "peel" from the orange heart girl's pocket.
2. By taking out their hearts/minds/souls with people who live there.

Hearts=hoUses

SOULS= cARs

Minds=schools

We live in our hearts.
We drive our souls.
We go to school in our minds.

Where people think they live:

Where people really live:

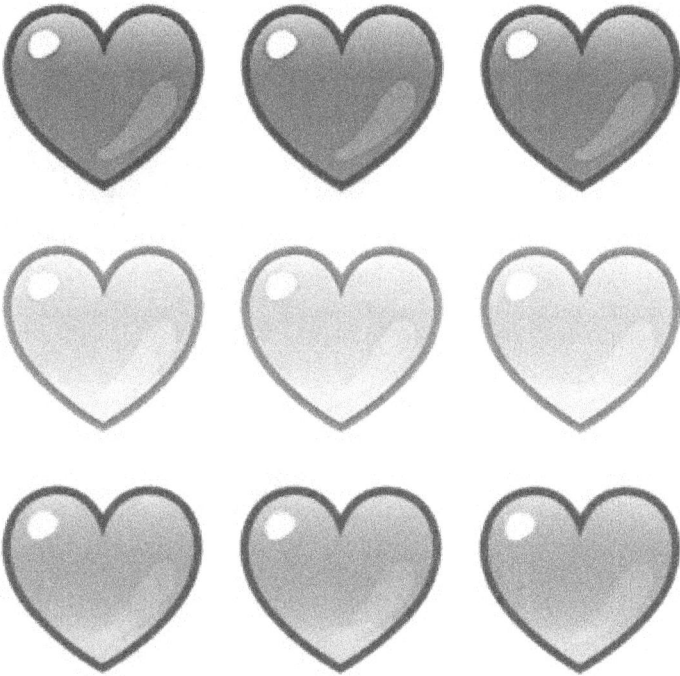

God puts on Her rain-bow before going to the graduation at the school of life:

Note -> To graduate life:
to put a thinking cap on you have to take off your child-hood.

Each girl takes something from their mind and puts

it on the cube:

Blue heart takes out a   s p
                         silver o
                                n o
Green heart puts a   p

              iece

        of cake.

(Society is a cake. You eat the bottom with a plastic fork and the top
with a silver spoon.)

Orange heart places a smoking

                    gun.

Do you love yourself is not a loaded question, but do you love
another person is.

Gold heart gives a   fish
        bowl
        fish

Red heart places a redherring.

Bronze heart places a key.

Silver heart gives a ven

ding

mach

ine.

White heart gives an icebErg.
(She cried, but her tears froze in her cold heart.)

Black heart gives a bitter pill.

lo
Yellow heart donates a g   b
e.

Purple heart gives a melting
pot.

fruit
Pink heart donates a forbidden
fruit.

Grey heart gives a drawing
board.

780 million people can't read the sentence:

I love you.

780 million people can't read the sentence:

I hate you.

We wear kisses.

We put on tears.

We drink emotions.

We eat feelings.

We take care of dreams.

We grow thoughts.

In the State of Mind:
Nightmares are millionaires &

dreams
live on welfare.

The 13 girls decide to celebrate their conquering of the ice cube, so they make emotions to get drunk on.

Drink & how it's made:

Red heart feeds loan sharks- red herrings, before cutting their fins to make shark fin soup. She cooks nothing, because she is arrested and then released for animal cruelty.

Orange heart milks a cash cow by threatening to shoot the cow with a smoking gun to produce greed.

Yellow heart pours all the tears from the globe into a paper cup to create pity.

Green heart puts a piece of cake through the gender blender to whip up equality.

Blue heart takes the silver spoon, uses it to mix a glass of liquid money and garnishes it with some trimmings from a hedge-fund. She makes greed. (If you swallow a silver spoon, you will lose your voice.)

Purple girl boils a tear in a melting pot to create anger. (You boil anger to kill toxic thoughts.)

Gold heart hires a gold digger to get the gold from the goldfish in the fishbowl, then mixes it with tears. She makes jealousy.

Silver heart steals honest-tea from a vending machine and makes dishones-tea.

Bronze heart opens a star with the key and bottles liquid fame. She produces infamy.

White heart melts the iceberg with a fire of love and ends up with water.

Grey heart is allergic to emotions.

Black heart dissolves the bitter pill in a cup of tears to end up with depression.

Pink heart squeezes a forbidden fruit to make lust.

love eats hunger.

Hunger is the food of love.

The two ways to leave a heart are:

1. **Clim**b down the social ladder

2. **Run** down the fire exit

We make the fire of love.

This is an image of life eating love.

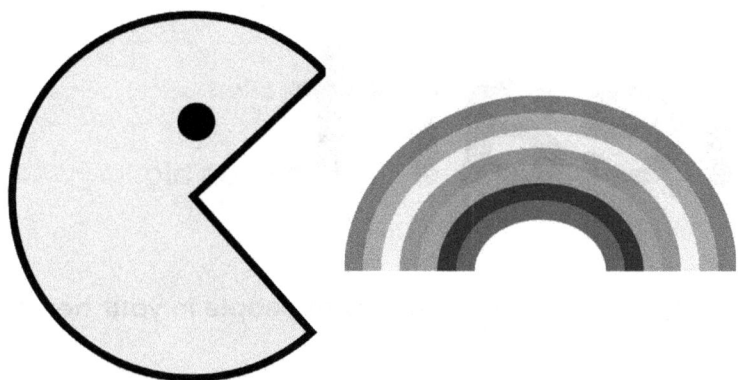

Happy relationship: fire of love 24/7

Abusive relationship:
The fire of love becomes the fire of hell.

People are rich, because they have
big hearts not houses.

I'm overweight because my

heart is too big.

The quality of your heart = quality of people in your heart

Hearts are countries bordered by **minds and populated by souls.** There are 7.5 billion countries on earth.

(Developed hearts give **love** to **developing hearts.)**

All humans are immigrants moving from heart to heart.

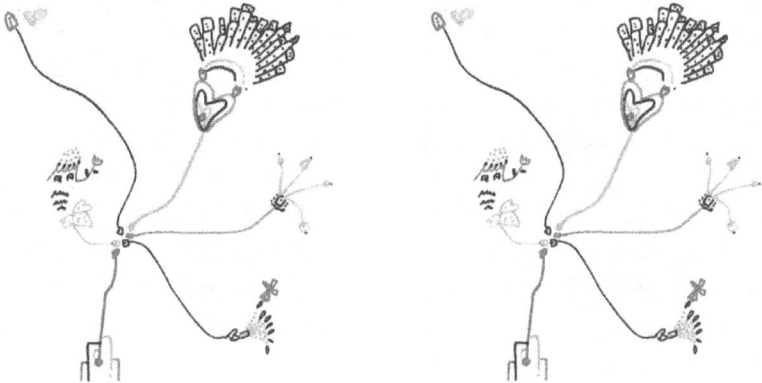

Immigrants to new hearts need to learn the language of love

The heart is an upside-down social pyramid

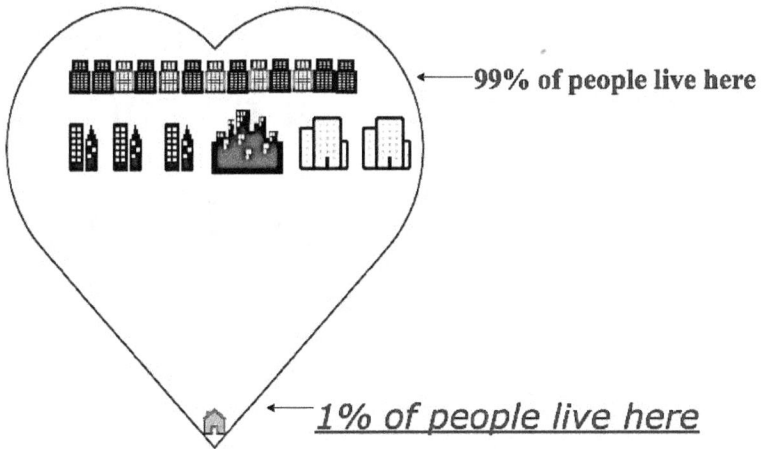

99% of people live here

1% of people live here

A random story that makes no sense at all:

English is a serial killer. He murders other languages. They become dead languages. He gets caught after leaving a foreign language in a comma. He gets a run-on sentence.

Another random story that makes no sense at all:

History has a sex change and a colour-change and becomes herstory. Then, herstory decides to just be a person and becomes every-story.

The girl with the blue heart leaves the cube. In the center of the ice cube is a Rubik's Cube. She hits the ice with her heart. Both break. On the Rubik's Cube is an aquarium of tears, dream farm and a museum of broken hearts.

THE GIRL WITH THE BLUE HEART walks into the aquarium and pays for admission and a boat ticket with **2 tears** and **a kiss.**

There are three boats on the River of Death:

Fear, Greed and oblivion.

THE GIRL WITH THE BLUE HEART boards the fear-

boat. The boat hits the **tree of life**.

Death swallows the river of death. The **afraid**/**greedy**/*forgetful* people become stuck in Death's heart.

Forgetful people grow forget-me-nots.

People with Greed grow weed.

People with Fear including THE GIRL WITH THE BLUE HEART, make beer. We get drunk on fear-beer, high on greed-weed and sober on honest-tea.

Stoners ~~erode~~ their consciences and die on cliff-hangers. The hammered people break the heart of Will with a middle of To and a last name of Live.

The *Forgetful* people continue to grow:

1. OffshOots
2. **Money**

    t

    r

    e

    e

    s

3.Hedge funds

Until the debt-pets eat everything
and the *Forgetful* people die in a

FOOD DESERT.

Green He-art

THE GIRL WITH THE GREEN HEART goes to the dream farm on the Rubik's cube.
There, she gets a job to plant memories, grow them into dreams & sell them to buy memories.

THE GIRL WITH THE GREEN HEART sells her roots for wings.

She trades her wings for a metal detector.

Finds a moral compass.

Walks to the north star.

The north star is only a mirror.

THE GIRL WITH THE GREEN HEART steps in.

Inside, everybody is a lock and she is the key that opens everybody's heart.

A PERSON TRIES TO OPEN THEIR MIND WITH THAT KEY. WHEN THEY CAN'T,

THEY LEAVE THE KEY ON A THOUGHT TRAIN.

Minds are stations for thought trains.

THE GIRL WITH
GOES TO THE
A RECYCLING
FACTORY AND
A LOCK.

THE GREEN HEART
LOST & FOUND, THEN
PLANT, THEN A
GETS TURNED INTO

A magician finds the lock and brings

THE GIRL WITH THE GREEN HEART back to life.

SHE moves to her mind and joins the army to fight

the war: Mind versus Heart, inside her.

Wars happen because of:
1. Money trees
2. Religion pigeons

[There are two wars inside you:

YOU AGAINST YOU and you against the world].

"THE GIRL WITH THE GREEN HEART dies, because

she had too many struggles," says

the mind side.

"THE GIRL WITH THE GREEN HEART dies, because

she carried too many dreams,"

says the heart side.

89

Life is a Box.

There are 2 ways to leave it:

1. Die

2. Do something awesome.

Pink He-art

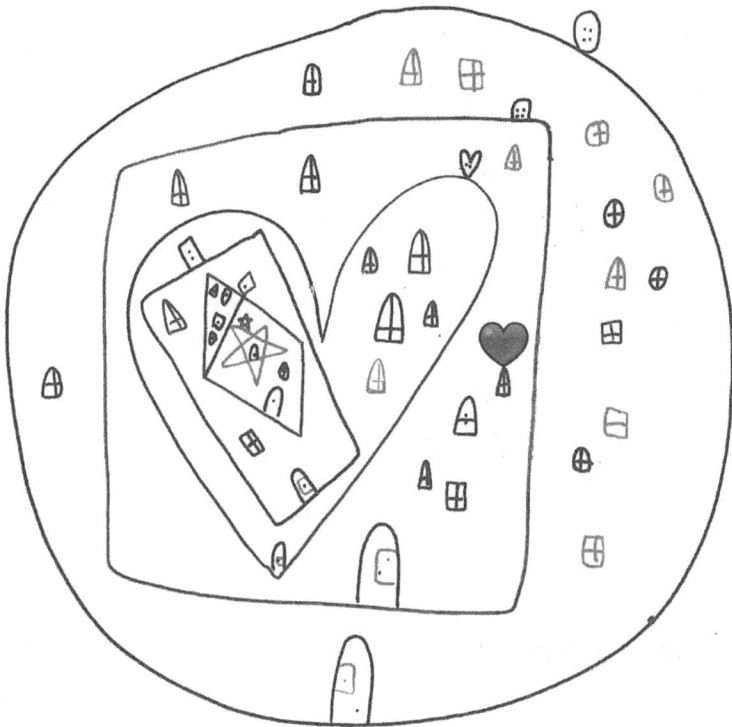

The girl with the pink heart goes inside the Rubik's cube to the museum of **bro rts**.
ken **hea**

Society is a box and my heart doesn't live there!

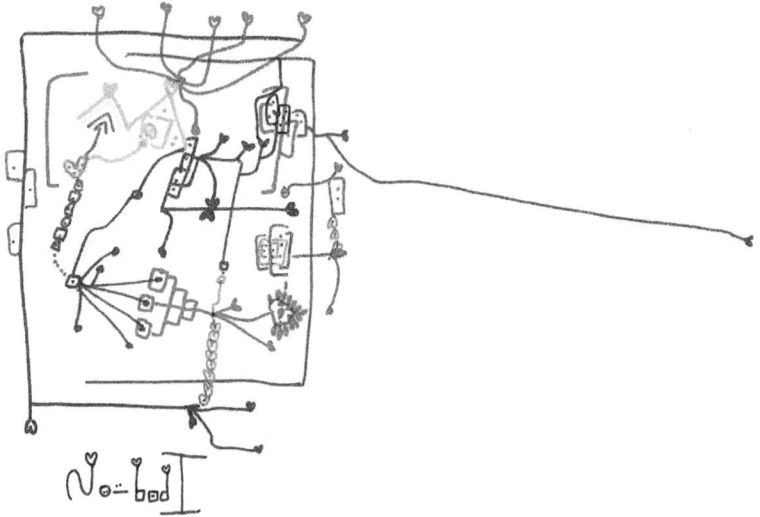

The girl with the pink heart steals the hearts from the exhibits, builds a city out of them and moves there. Nobody lives there except a flower, who lives on a psycho-path. The girl and the flower both try to break into a heart and get stuck trying to leave.

In the heart, there is only a word-knife and not enough dreams to survive.

The flower tries to stab her with the word dog, but a week later she cuts herself with the word "God" and dies.

The flower spends days screaming, but nobody hears him, because there is nobody else in the city.

The flower breaks the heart with the word: mind.

The flower leaves the city and goes to the dream police.

The flower moves to a word-ward, thanks to a sentence.

The flower looks in a mirror, realizes he is a rose, falls in love with the world, and dies in love with the world.

The girls, except the girl with the red heart, collect dreams from the people they knew/know/will know.

They build a dream wall.

It separates: the dreams from the nightmares.

Red He-art

The girl with the red heart wrote on the wall with her **VOICE**:

"Life is a tri**a**ngle, not a ci**rc**le. It has a point."

She destroys the **wall** and finds a gun store which sells words. She buys a
loaded
question.

The woman, called Eternity, next to the girl with the red heart **wants a *naked truth*.** The cashier gives Eternity a `white lie`. When Eternity tries to commit suicide, instead of shooting a word-bullet, a dove flies away.

`The dove`

d
o
v
e

into the war

the

world

wore.

Don't chase the
`love-dove`
away from the
square of life.

Don't let
the religion
pigeon kill the
`love-dove.`

The girl with the red heart finds Time on the s t r e e t.

He is washing the brains of **immortal** people.

The girl with the red heart kills Time with a loaded
question.

Then, the girl with the red heart is caught by the dream police and put into a

blood cell.

She shares it with the trillions of people who would have been created instead of her. At the trial, she is acquitted of having ever lived, because Time doesn't exist no more.

everybody is a . not a ,

everybody is a ! not a ?

everybody is a [ ] not a ( )

Human Evolution*:

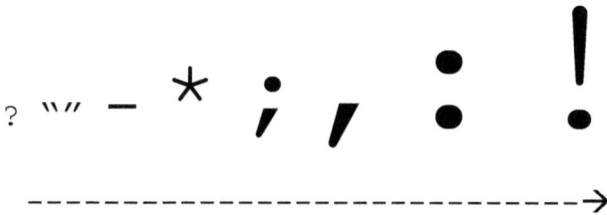

? \" — * ; , : !
-------------------------------→

*We are question marks, then quotation marks,
then dashes, then asterisks, then semi colons,
then commas, then colons, then exclamation
marks.

Human De-evolution:

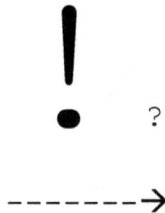

!
•   ?

-------→

* We are exclamation marks, then question
marks because we question our existence by
validating our existence.

The girl with the red heart takes an

elev

ator to the **glass ceiling**.

In the elevator, she rides with:

1.The first guy who painted the ==white house== black.

It was repainted white.

2.The first woman, who almost broke ~~the glass~~

~~ceiling.~~

Everybody gets out at the

level

under the

glass ceiling,

except the girl with the red heart.

RANDOM SUICIDE STATISTICS:
1. 1,000,000 PEOPLE HANG THEMSELVES FROM THE
GLASS CEILING EVERY YEAR.
2. 1,000,001 PEOPLE JUMP FROM THE GLASS CEILING
EVERY YEAR. *SOURCE: LIFE*

On the ceiling is a white

HOUSe,

but admission is a dollar, and she has
only 78 cents.

The girl with the red heart tries to
jump
  over
    the pay gap to get to the white house,

but she falls
        down

and lands in the sands of time.

Using the fire in her belly, she melts the sand into glass and builds a glass tower taller than the glass ceiling.

Everybody on the ice cube moves to the top of the tower and they construct a black/brown/white/red/yellow house on top.

The glass ceiling

becomes a floor.

And the girl with the red heart spends the

rest of her life sweeping and cleaning it. (just kidding)

We are races, classes, genders, sexualities, trying to break

the feeling-ceiling

and become emotions.

Purple He-art

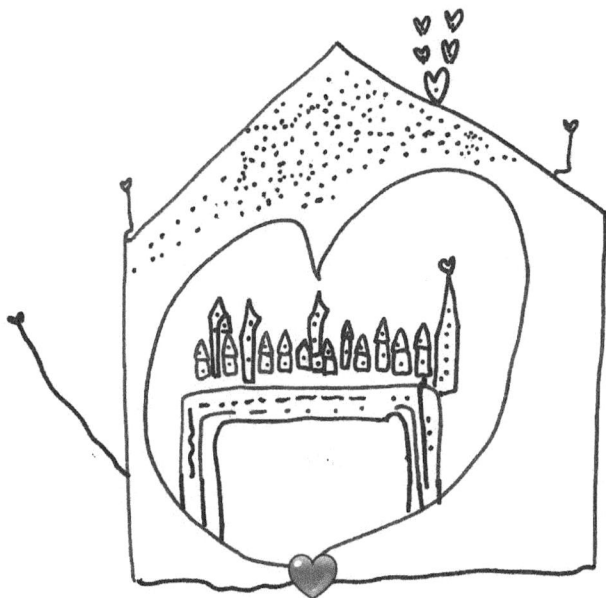

On the ice-cube, the girl with the purple heart builds a pet shop in her heart.

Ambitions are dogs in blue/white/pink/orange and no collars.

When people buy ambitions, the girl with the purple heart is forced by society to give them collars.

One day, **virtual** ambitions are discovered.

Robots begin to wear **virtual ambitions** with **virtual** collars.

Soon every ambition is **virtual.**

When people can't find ambitions, their hearts go searching for them and get lost.

The girl with the purple heart converts the store into a shelter for lost hearts.

In her heart inside a rib-cage, hearts live and die in their rib-cages.

I Lost my Mind, so I Moved to my Heart

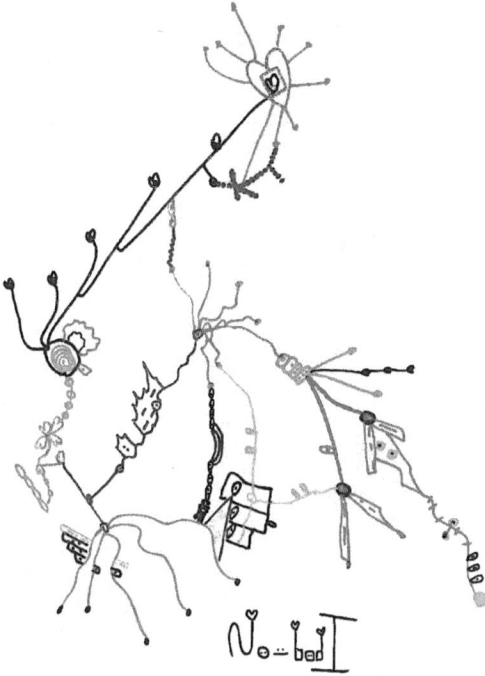

Life is a house

and love is a home

Death   takes   the
highway of life:

He stops at a

Hotel: 🩶

Inn: 💘

Apartment: 💕

Motel: 💔

Hostel: 🩷

On the ice-cube, Death finds TIME

hanging from a clock and shot to death

(by the girl with the red heart).

 to a .

He tries all the free numbers:

Death calls:

The heart-fire station, because his heart is burning.

The mind–ambulance station, because his mind is sick.

The soul-police station, because his soul is lost.

Random Personal notes:
When I was depressed, I kept a journal:
Here are the best thoughts from it:

Life is a `hospital` filled with bro-ken hearts and `sick` minds.

Most common reason a heart breaks:
You break your heart and blame it on someone else.

How to avoid a __sick mind__

__feed your mInd__
__books so it__
__doesn't__
__get sick__

cost of phone calls
(at the payphone where Death is):

Paid numbers	Cost
To Someone living in the past	1 dream
To Someone living in the present	1 thought
To Someone living in the future	1 memory

Using 1 dream, Death calls Eternity, **since Eternity is Time's widow.** She picks up, and Death tells her: "**Time didn't kill Time**".

The police, fire and ambulance come to the phone and take Death's heart, mind & soul, and Death goes back to Hell.

He'll go to Hell.   (Death)

She'll be a shell.   (Eternity)

We'll be a well.   (humanity)

Eternity buries Time in the fountain of youth. She then tries to kill herself every way possible, but she is immortal, so she tries to build a card tower in her mind. Kings and queens visit her mind, each playing the game of love with her, until she realizes that everybody cheated, and she is only a joker.

Life is a game:

50% of people play chess   50 % of people play checkers.

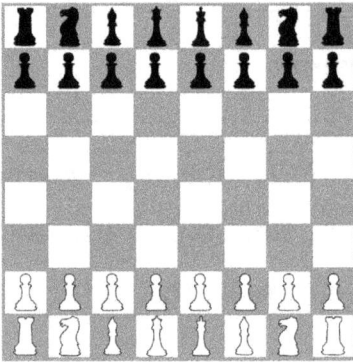

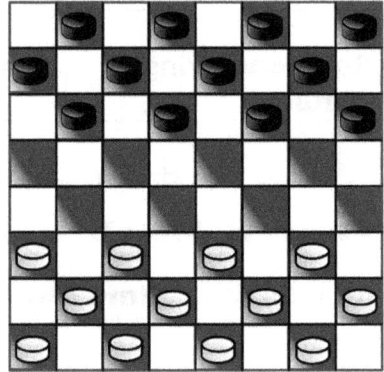

Eternity moves from her mind to her heart. To be able to pay the rent that life charges, she has two roommates: Love and Hate. Love is an arsonist and Hate is a firefighter. Eternity's heart gets smaller, and she has to evict somebody.

She thinks Hate is setting the fires and kicks him out. Love burns everything in Eternity's heart, except a trump card. Love moves to another heart, and to another one, until she burns her own heart.

lust sews kisses. love sows kisses.

lust reigns hearts. love rains hearts.

lust needs love. love kneads love.

People go to the different sides of the ice cube.

On Side 1, everybody has *wings.*

On Side 2, everybody has <u>roots.</u>

On Side 3, everybody rubs **hearts.**

On Side 4, everybody washes BRAINS.

On Side 5, everybody runs out of dreams.

On Side 6, everybody fights over a flower.

The 6 sides on the ice-cube:

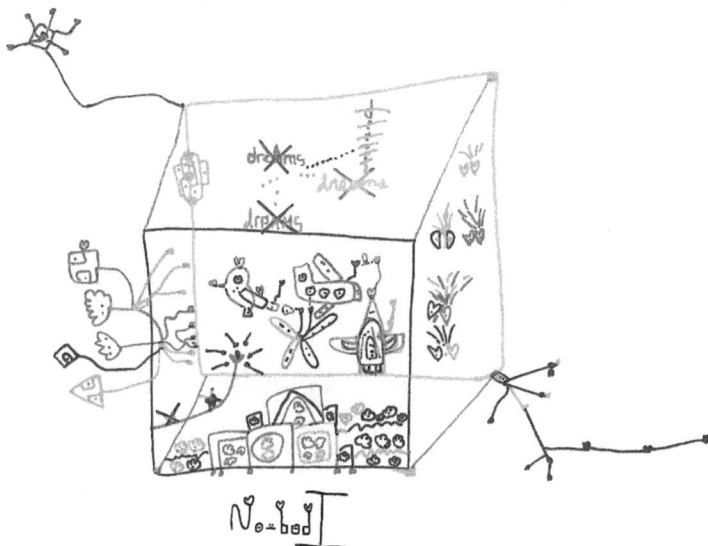

On the side where everybody has Wings:

The younger birds clip ~~the~~ Wings of the older birds, and then the older birds clip ~~the~~ Wings of the younger birds.

fly
The birds who can   evolve into lame ducks, because every kid with Wings can become grounded.

Since you are made from the
birdS and the bees

you are my **honey**

and **WingS**.

Half of humans are **birdS** and half are TRE

E

S

.

We either give up our roOts or **WingS**.

Half of people have wings:

Can fly the highest:

brain-planes (smart people)

can fly:

**social butterflies/wasps
(extroverts/upper class)**

can't fly:

lame ducks/ mother hens
(morally weak people/some parents)

Chicken/**egg** scenario: does life **or** love come first?

 vs  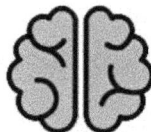 vs

111

Half of people have roots:

coun-tree = nationalists

artis-tree = artists

chemis-tree = scientists

off-shoo t= entrepreneurs

bigo-tree = bigots :(

On the side where everybody has roOts:

Everybody has roots connected to a coun-tree. except those who don't.

PEOPLE LIVE IN 196 GROUPS:
GROUP 1-195: 195 COUN-TREES
GROUP 196: TREE-LESS

But in reality, the coun-trees are cardboard and the "trees" eventually disintegrate.

People plant a tree of life, but it creates more coun-trees.

THE COUN-TREES CREATE BIGO-TREES.
THE BIGO-TREES GROW HATE-FRUITS. *

The people who give fruits from the bigo-trees die on the outside.
The people who receive fruits from the bigo-trees die on the inside.

*NOTHING TO DO WITH THE HURTFUL SLANG

On the side where people were rubbing

heartshearts:

FOR THE OPTIMIST:
EVERY HEART BREAKS AND THE FIRES STOP, UNTIL SOME
GIRL DISCOVERS, THAT TWO BROKEN HALVES OF A HEART
CAN MAKE A LOVE-FIRE TOO.

For the pessimist:
One girl discovers ice in her heart.
She gives it to everybody.
Instead of rubbing their hearts
everybody is freezing them.

For the idealist:
Everybody keeps rubbing their hearts, so they fuse and become a
single heart.

For the realist:
Everybody keeps rubbing their hearts, so they all
break.

A heart for a heart makes the world broken*.
(*Gandhi paraphrase*)

Scientific Results of trying to make a heart fire:

Heart and key = open relationship

+ =

Heart and lock = closed relationship

+ =

Heart and matches = arranged relationship

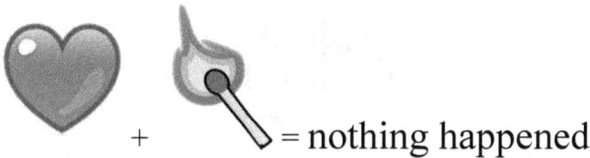

+ = nothing happened

On the side where people are washing brains:

THE LAUNDROMAT, CALLED SOCIETY, CAN'T BRAINWASH ANYMORE, BECAUSE IT RUNS OUT OF POWER.
(Society washes our brains before it fries them.)

People take back their minds.

Then, Life gives them tears, so they begin drowning tears instead.

Brains when washed by setting:

Delicate: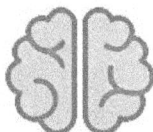

Heavy: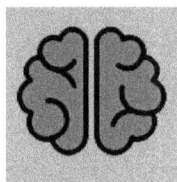

Normal: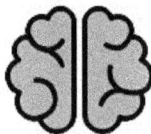

White: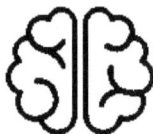

On the side where everybody ran out of dreams: **THEY FIND NIGHT-MARES.**

EVERYBODY BUILDS FARMS IN THEIR MINDS FOR THE NIGHT-MARES. IN EVERY MIND, EVERY NIGHT-MARE GIVES BIRTH TO A DARK-HORSE OR A DRUG-MULE.

A Night-mare can give birth to a:

Dark horse:

Stud:

Work-horse:

Night-mare:

Drug mule:

life is a **farm**:

queen bee:

cash cow:

lame duck:

drug mule:  **work horse:** **scapegoat:**

love is a ~~zoo~~:

butterfly in the stomach:

crocodile tear*

 lone wolf

*crocodile tears are endangered

See a sea.

Be a bee.

Beat a beet.

See a sea.

Be a bee.

Beat a beet.

See a sea.

Be a bee.

Beat a beet.

See a sea.

Be a bee.

Beat a beet.

See a sea.

Be a bee.

Beat a beet.

ON THE SIDE WHERE EVERYBODY FIGHTS OVER A FLOWER CALLED FAME:
1. EVERYBODY'S HEART AND MIND   FIGHT.
2. EVERYBODY'S HEARTS AND MINDS FIGHT.

Gold He-art

We sought what **we fought**. **We fought** what we sought.

At night, the girl with the gold heart takes the flower of fame and leaves a mirror in its place. Then, she puts the flower of fame on suicide watch, but it dies 15 minutes later. In the morning, everybody looks at the mirror and finds a garden in their hearts. They go into their hearts to look for the flower of fame, but it can't grow in hearts, only in minds. There, in their hearts, they discover their family trees and decide to live on them instead of looking for the flower of fame.

 = family tree  = flower of fame

Life is:

Seeds of existence grow into family trees.

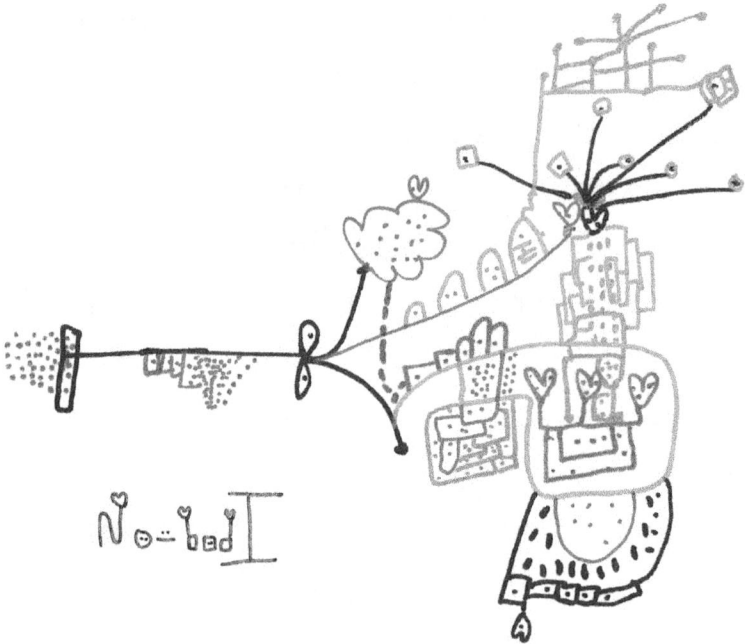

Money trees grow on river banks.

Family trees grow on blood-streams.

The mind says:
money tree> family tree

The heart thinks:
family tree> money tree

Cash cows eat money trees. The kids of cash cows are bull markets.

We hide from bear markets by climbing on money trees.

The family tree of every heart

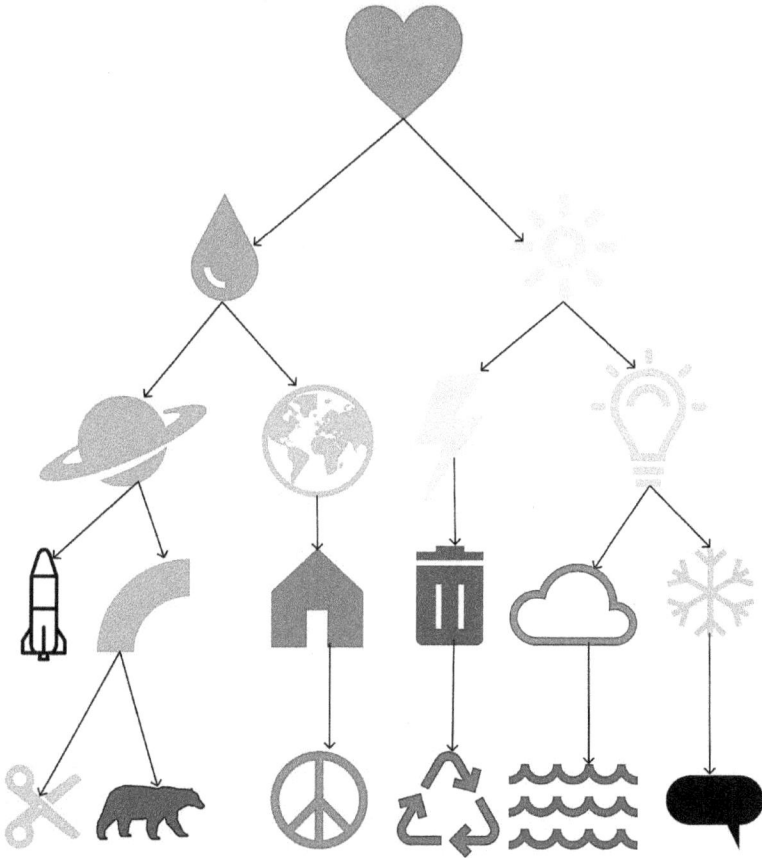

Because more people begin to make love-fires using family trees, the ice-cube turns into a water-square. The planet becomes a lake of people, and when people begin to cry- a sea of people.

Bronze He-art

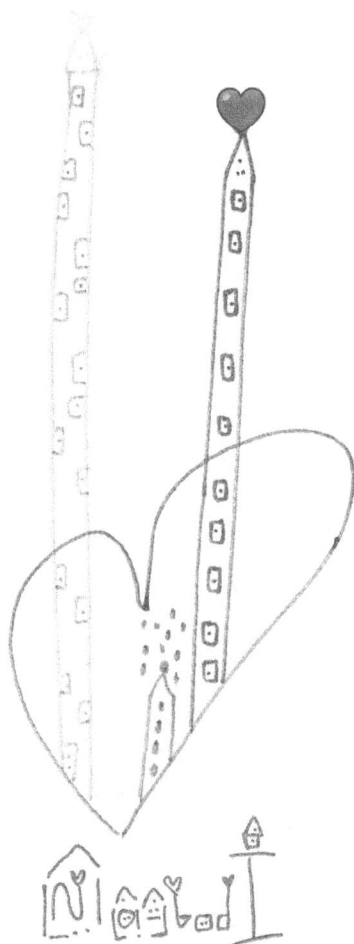

The girl with the bronze heart wants to go to the **FOUNTAIN OF YOUTH,** but she walks to the **fountain of old-age** instead.

People who throw coins into the fountain of youth dig them out to pay for the ferry of death.

The girl with the bronze heart drinks from the **fountain of old-age,** becomes old, and goes to Heaven.

Silver

He-
art

The girl with the silver heart goes to the gene pool in her **gen**

E s.

She takes divin

g lessons and then jumps

in.

Soon, the girl with the silver heart travels across the Universe, creating more and more gene pools. She hires angels for lifeguards. The capacity for each pool is 46 chromosomes, until the girl decides to change the capacity to any number of swimmers (between 45 and 49). What happens to her afterwards is unknown.

The girl with the gold heart makes it to the river of death (Death had swallowed it but it formed again). She falls in. She pretends to be dead, but the river continues into a factory. In the factory of reincarnation, there is a machine that transforms living beings into new ones.

The girl with the gold heart becomes a man with a blue mind. He goes through the river again and again, and becomes an animal, then an insect, then a plant, then a bacterium, and then a plant, and then an insect, and then an animal, then a man with a blue mind, and finally, a girl with the gold heart.

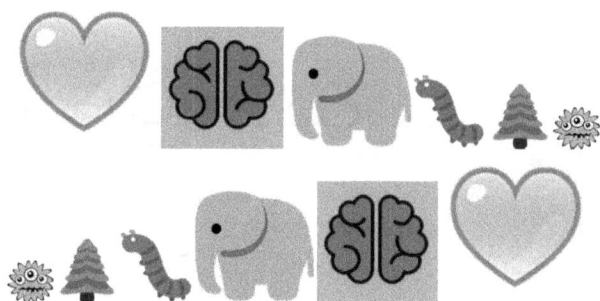

The girl with the gold heart gets a job at the factory of reincarnation, marries herself, has an abusive relationship, and finally divorces herself.

She goes through the machine one more time and becomes an angel.

Nobody can use a *straightener* on your soul. So, use your an-gel.

The girl with the orange heart **is asked to cook war.** She **doesn't know how to cook, so** she **serves it raw. [A raw war is a revolution.]** The girl with the orange heart **boils her anger and makes a war.** She **becomes a dictator.**

When there are elections in your heart vote for yourself.

You are the king/queen/president/dictator of your heart.

You are also the peasant/homeless

person/factory worker/farmer (there).

Everybody becomes shallow, so the sea of people dries up, and people move to her heart. There, they find an inhospitable desert. Everybody breaks her heart to get out, and she dies alone on the phone on the throne on the stone in the zone.

The sea of people forms again, (because people cry), but soon splits up into several lakes, then rivers, streams, and, eventually, puddles. The puddles evaporate.

IT RAINS WOMEN/ SNOWS MEN/HAILS NON-BINARY PEOPLE TONIGHT.

IT RAINS WOMEN

♀ ⚥♀ ♀ ⚥⚧♀ ⚥♀

♀ ⚥♀ ♀ ⚥⚧♀ ⚥♀

IT SNOWS MEN

♂ ♂♂⚤⚥♂♂⚥♂

♂ ♂♂⚤⚥♂♂⚥♂

IT HAILS NON-BINARY PEOPLE

☿ ○ ⚲ ⚨ ♀ ⚩

☿ ○ ⚲ ⚨ ♀ ⚩

THEY ALL LAND IN THE SEA OF PEOPLE:

♂♂♀♀○⚥♂♀○⚥☿⚨⚲♀○☿⚲○⚨☿⚥♂♂♂⚥♂♂♂♀⚥♂

AND BECOME HEARTS:

💚🤎🧡💚💔💚💜💘💛🤍🖤💕💚

🤍🤎💛💔💚🖤💕🖤💕💚🖤💕💚

No-bodI

Which person is different?

Answer: You reading this.

The girl with the yellow heart

Builds a **BOMB OUT OF WORDS.**

She destroys the city of life.

The girl with the yellow heart

Builds a **BOMB OUT OF SILENCE.**

She destroys the city of death .

(Death dies in the city of death.)

~~Death is dead.~~

Hate is hated.

Fear is afraid.

Anger is angry.

Love is in love.

Everyone is stranded on the highway of life.

If you **sell hell**

you can **lease peace.**

Earth/Hell/Heaven reviews:

Earth ★★★★★/10 based on 7.5 billion reviews

A random review: ★★

The world is an oyster. I tried to eat it, but I am a vegetarian. (So, I put it back in the ocean.)

Hell ★★★★★★/10 based on 1 review

A random review: ★★★★★★

I dwell in hell wearing gel in my cell after the bell about whether to sell my soul and become a shell so that I can drink from the well and to be able to tell the wardens not to yell; otherwise, Hell is swell.

Heaven ★★★★★★/10 based on 2 reviews

A random review: ★★

Heaven is not accessible as the ramp isn't built yet.

Another random review: ★★★★★★★★★

I took the escalator up from the top of the glass ceiling to heaven. Only available to 1/100 people.

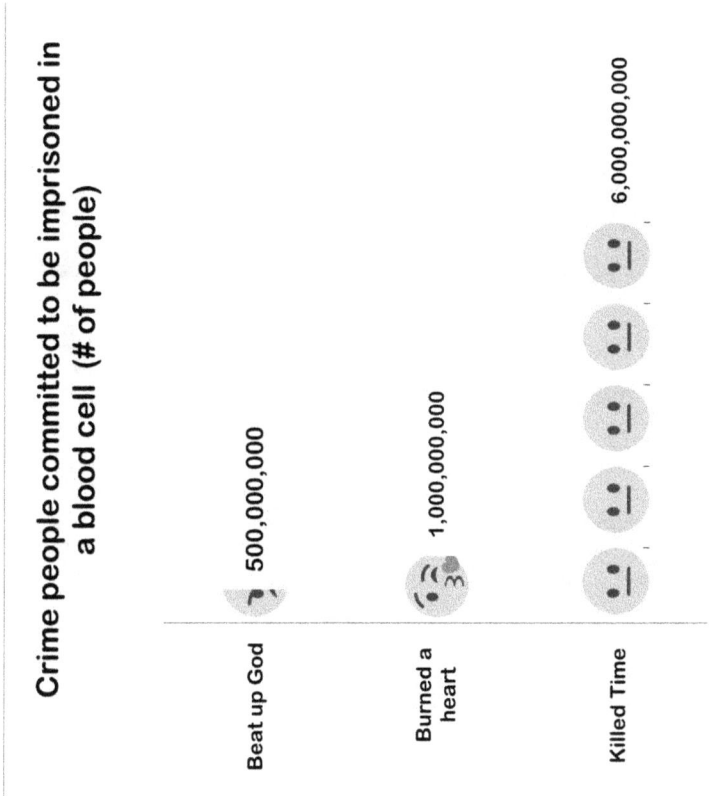

Crime people committed to be imprisoned in a blood cell (# of people)

500,000,000 — Beat up God

1,000,000,000 — Burned a heart

6,000,000,000 — Killed Time

note: (approx. 500,000,000 atheists in the world)

We wear **genes** in blood cells.

135

You are a house

You are
not your
wiring

You are a house

You are not your
paint

You are not
your plumbing

You are a house

You are a house.

God invites everybody to Her house due to the chaos. Her home is divided by:

a glass ceiling, a **poverty line**,

an iron|curtain, and has a

clo

set

God's House

Random photo collage:

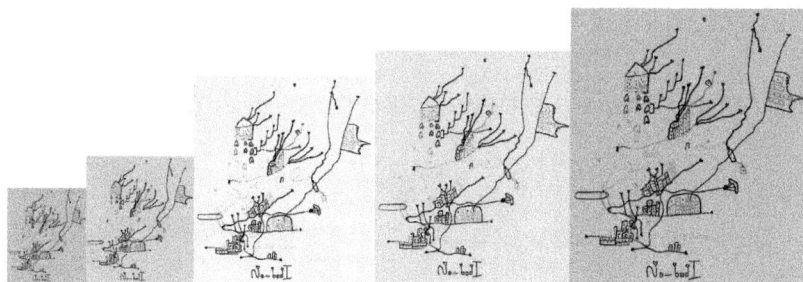

Some people move under the glass ceiling, but above the poverty line. Some people are in the closet, under the iron curtain, and the glass ceiling, and beneath the poverty line. Some people can/will never see that there was a closet or a poverty line or a glass ceiling, or an iron curtain, as they sit on the prive-ledge and decide how the world should change, when everybody else just wants to change the world just as much as them.

The girl with the yellow heart trips over the poverty line, bumps her head on the glass ceiling and falls into a closet where she suffocates.

You play life with a preju-dice on a prive-ledge.

God leaves Her house to discover parallel universes.

In parallel universe 1: she is a <u>human.</u>

In parallel universe 2: she is a <u>human.</u>

In parallel universe 3: she is <u>human.</u>

In parallel universe 10: she is <u>human.</u>

In parallel universe 100: she is a <u>human.</u>

In parallel universe 1000: she is a <u>human.</u>

In parallel universe 7,500,000,000: she is a <u>human.</u>

In this universe: she is an **object**.

When God got home she destroyed all the barriers
in her house and made everybody:
a moneyless, race-less, asexual,
country-less, genderless being.

Everybody moves onto the ground floor of
God's house around the circle of life.

Then, God goes to write the *Test of Life* ™.

She scribbles Her name on the front of the test:
Absolute Spirit Absolute Consciousness Absolute
Inclusiveness Absolute Allah Anima Mundi Atman Black
Madonna Brahma Buddha Causal Causeless Cause Chi Christ
Christ Consciousness Cosmic Christ Consciousness Conscious
Universe Divine Divine Feminine Divine   Mother
Divine Mystery Divine Presence Divine
Providence Elan Vital Ein Sof Eshwara   Ever
Present Origin Evolution Evolutionary   Spirit
                Evolution Spirituality Gaia God Godde
Goddess   Great Consciousness Great I Am Great
               Interconnectedness Great Mother Great
Mystery   Great Spirit Great Union Great Unity
Great Unfolding Great Radiance Great Relationship Higher
Power Highest Essence Highest Self Holy Spirit I am Who am
Infinite Consciousness Infinite Essence Infinite Mystery
Infinite one Infinite oneness Infinite Source Infinite
Spirit Infinite Wholeness Integrative Consciousness
Integrative Spirit Jehovah Jesus Kali Kosmos Krishna Larger
Self Love   Mary (Drugs and Jesus have the same
mom.)   Mother Universe Nameless One Nondual
Awareness   OM Original Essence Original
Organizing   Principle Oya Pele Post Big Bang
Reality Prana Pre Big Bang Reality Shakti Shiva The Cosmos
The Great Oneness The Source The Eternal Now The Everything
and the Nothing The Evolutionary Absolute The Evolutionary
Union The Flow of Life or Life Force The Infinite The Good
The Great Spirit The Tao The Great Unified
Field The Force The Tripartite Absolute The
Absolute Trinity The Supreme The Union The
Unity The Universe Itself The Universal One
The Ultimate The Universe or Living Universe The Universal
or Universe Source, Spirit or Soul Total Reality Total Pre
and Post Big Bang Reality Total Universe Reality The
Wholeness of the Universe Ultimate Concern Ultimate Reality
Ultimate Universe Reality Ultimate Truth Ultimate Unity or
Oneness Ultimate Wholeness Universe Consciousness Universe
Entity Universal Life Universal Oneness Universal Soul
Vishnu World Soul Yahweh YHWH Wakan Taka
(but she forgets a couple names)

Name: ___ (unless you are one of the 780 million that can't write it,)

The Test of Life™:

True or false:

Every person is equal ___

Fill in the blank:

Every person is _____

Choices: equal or unequal.

Multiple choice:

Every person is: ____

A. Equal

B: Unequal

God didn't answer any test questions.

**Then, God decides to legally change
Her NAME to Human. Because GOD is a Human.**

*The girls with the white, grey, black hearts leave
Human's house and split up.*

∩↓←⇨ ↓▽ ↘⇨⇔⇨ ▶▲ ↕←
Life is made up of

↓↔   in

←↕△↗▽◀↑⇨ forks the   ⇨↔⇔

△↕⇨⇔   road   **&**

▽↙↓▲   **slip**

▲⇨△◢   **pery**

▽↙↕▲⇨▽↘   **slopes**

←↕◀   ⇨△⇨↑◥◀ ◢▲⇨▽↘

not   archetypes.

Black He-art

The girl with the black heart walks West <-. She gets to a slippery slope. She tries to graph the trajectory of her Life, but then she realizes, her life is an equation, not a graph. (Because math/STEM can be *x and x just* as much as *x and y*.) She spends her life climbing up the slope, hitting her head on the glass ceiling at the, falling down, and continuing this cycle for all eternity.

The girl with the white heart travels East ->. She reaches a fork in the road. She uses it to eat her problems, struggles, frustrations, issues until she chokes when she tries to consume her dreams. (When you get to a fork in the road use it to eat your problems.) Her last thought is that she is happy.

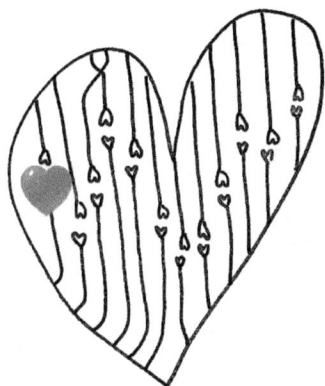

Grey He-art

Grey He-art

The girl with the grey heart heads North. She walks past a voice box/a blood cell/a rib cage until she enters a snow globe. She finds nobody there, so she spends her life alternating between an ice queen and a snow angel.
The girl with the grey heart heads North. She walks past a voice box/a blood cell/a rib cage until she enters a snow globe. She finds nobody there, so she spends her life alternating between a snow angel and an ice queen.

We Drown in the river of death.
We Drown in the river of death.

Beverage Options on the Ferry of Death:

Ice queen™

Snow Angel™

Gator-rade

ice water

snow water

crocodile tears

frozen heart water

tear water

water

liquid money

human tears

juice

black sheep milk

boiled anger

beverage options on the ferry of death

milk

scapegoat milk

smoothie

beer

cash cow milk

work horse milk

tea

fear-beer

pover-tea

not fair trade

tear-beer

socie-tea

*daily special made in the gender blender

generosi-tea

cruel-tea

digni-tea

integri-tea

morali-tea

fair trade

identi-tea

inequali-tea

humili-tea

diversi-tea

hones-tea

pari-tea

liber-tea

equali-tea

In Human's house, everybody realizes the **Universe** is e.n.d.i.n.g. They put their life goal in a box.

4 billion people put a

piece of bread.

2 billion people put a **pen.**

1 billion people put a **tampon.**

500 million people put a **condom.**
1 person puts a ring.
1 person puts a weight scale.
1 person puts a measuring tape.
1 person puts a video game.
1/2 person puts a dove
1/2 a person puts a gun.

They leave the box in the sands of time and look up/down at the **Universe**.

They build the Tower of Babble, and in doing so all learn to speak Love.

Human leaves the moon and turns off the lights of the Universe. She climbs up to the **Tower of Babble** and **jumps.**

The movie of your life is based on the book of your destiny. The movie of life will end. The crew will take down the

cardboard stars,

clay planets,

paper sky,

cardboard people,

and will leave an empty Universe with nothing & nobody there.

To the reader:

You parked your soul in my mind on your windshield and I left the following:

1. A Custody Notice:
We all have custody of the Earth.

2. A Menu:
individuali-tea>conformi-tea

3. A Termination Letter:
Anger is firing us.

4. A Job Offer:
Peace is hiring us.

5. Divorce papers:
Divorce Hate.

6. A Marriage Proposal:
Marry Love.

7. A Peace Treaty:
Sadness has surrendered.

8. A Ransom note:
Society kidnapped your dreams. Get them back.

You walk back to your soul, read the things on the dashboard, drive your soul and get back to your mind.

There, you decide to buy a house.
There are 8 houses available:

If you buy the:

 u = sad    u = mad

 u = mad    u = sad

 u = sad    u = glad

 u = glad    u = sad

You buy the blue house.

You walk inside the house, turn on the TV and try to watch the movie of your life, but it is deleted.

Because life didn't care enough to save the movie.
Because life didn't care enough to save the movie.

Because you didn't let life care enough to save the movie.

LET LIFE CARE ENOUGH TO SAVE THE MOVIE. LET LIFE CARE ENOUGH TO REMEMBER YOU.

Acknowledgments

Thanks to my parents, my sister and my dog for supporting me.

Thanks to Prof Daniela Elza for editing this book.

Lighthouse image is from
https://upload.wikimedia.org/wikipedia/commons/thumb/9/9b/Lighthouse_icon.svg/
1024px-Lighthouse_icon.svg.png , band mate is from
https://upload.wikimedia.org/wikipedia/commons/c/ca/Band_Silhouette_06.jpg and
person walking is from
https://upload.wikimedia.org/wikipedia/commons/thumb/f/fe/Q25443024_noun_351
66_ccPierre-LucAuclair_to_walk.svg/2000px-Q25443024_noun_35166_ccPierre-
LucAuclair_to_walk.svg.png ©Wikipedia

Emojis are from ©Emojidex emoji ©emojidex https://www.emojidex.com and
©Twitter (©Twemojis), except for the emojis on the Life is a Farm, and Love is a Zoo
page, which were made by me using ©MojiShop and the brain image which was
taken from ©Draw IO.

Diagrams (melting pot, beverage flow chart, how to avoid a sick mind) are made on
©Draw IO and ©Create (diet of miracles, family tree of every heart) which is an IPad
app.

Gender, Sexuality, checkmark are ©Unicode symbols.

Graph (Crime committed) was made using Excel.

List of God names is from ©http://universespirit.org/.

The fact that 780 Million are illiterate comes from an article titled "Atlassian and
Room to Read Have Raised $3M to Help Educate Children in Developing Countries
on Tech" from ©TechCrunch by Catherine Su

Heart outline, fonts, colors, patterns, table templates are made with ©Microsoft
Word.

Car image is from http://www.freestockphotos.biz/stockphoto/15685 and fedora
image is from http://res.freestockphotos.biz/pictures/15/15577-illustration-of-a-
brown-cartoon-hat-pv.png ©Free Stock Photos Biz

Emoticon Symbols are from
http://www.netlingo.com/more/NetLingo_List_of_Emoticons.pdf ©Netlingo and
https://whitefiles.org/b1_s/1_free_guides/fg2cd/pgs/f02_emtcns.htm © The White
Files.

Number of atheists in the world is from "The Demographics of Atheism" ©Wikipedia
Page.

The Cartoon Table is from: http://www.how-to-draw-funny-
cartoons.com/images/xcartoon-table6.gif.pagespeed.ic.VI3JnNHra0.png
© How to draw funny cartoons

Note: All drawings are made by NobodI (which is another pen name of Ideas with Ink).

About the Author:

Ideas with Ink is the pseudonym of a teenage author from Canada. Please check out his first poetry book "Time Capsule", the children's books "The Dragon in the Glass Ball" and "The Tiger Family Stories: Story One: Why Am I Vegetarian?" (in collaboration with Mama Bear)

Note: You can contact the author by e-mail at ideaswithink@gmail.com

Please: Follow on IG, FB, G+ and Tw @ideaswithink

About the person:

I'm a hue-man.
I'm a hue-man.
I'm a hue-man.
I'm a hue-man.
I'm a hue-man.
I'm a hue-man.
I'm a hue-man.
I'm a hue-man.
I'm a hue-man.
I'm a hue-man.
I'm a hue-man.
I'm a hue-man.
I'm a hue-man.
I'm a hue-man.
I'm a hue-man.
I'm a hue-man.
I'm a human.

About me:

:(I drew butterflies on my arms. The butterflies needed flowers to stay alive. The flowers needed bees. The bees needed trees. The trees needed rivers. And so on. I drew the whole cycle of nature on my arms. I drew rain when I was sad and sun when I was happy. I did this for a month and then I was sad and I decided to draw objects, on my arms because I felt like an object. On my arms, I drew a ship, and a house, and a train and a car, and a city, and streetlamps and laptops, and textbooks, and coffee cups and shirts, and a mannequin. I made the mannequin a person. I gave the person purple skin, a green mind and a blue heart. This became the girl with the blue heart. The girl with the blue heart got a blue castle, and a blue ship, and a blue coat. Then I started to draw in my notebook and write this book on my laptop. :)